Animals Close Up

CATS CLOSE UP

By Seth Lynch

Gareth Stevens
PUBLISHING

Please visit our website, www.garethstevens.com. For a free color catalog of all our high-quality books, call toll free 1-800-542-2595 or fax 1-877-542-2596.

Library of Congress Cataloging-in-Publication Data
Names: Lynch, Seth, author.
Title: Cats close up / Seth Lynch.
Description: New York : Gareth Stevens Publishing, [2023] | Series: Animals close up | Includes index.
Identifiers: LCCN 2021040547 (print) | LCCN 2021040548 (ebook) | ISBN 9781538281208 (set) | ISBN 9781538281215 (library binding) | ISBN 9781538281192 (paperback) | ISBN 9781538281222 (ebook)
Subjects: LCSH: Cats–Juvenile literature.
Classification: LCC SF445.7 .L97 2023 (print) | LCC SF445.7 (ebook) | DDC 636.8–dc23
LC record available at https://lccn.loc.gov/2021040547
LC ebook record available at https://lccn.loc.gov/2021040548

First Edition

Published in 2023 by
Gareth Stevens Publishing
29 East 21st Street
New York, NY 10010

Editor: Kristen Nelson
Designer: Rachel Rising

Photo credits: Cover, p.1 Alena Ozerova/Shutterstock.com; p. 5 Tobyanna/Shutterstock.com; p. 7 Dmitry Syshchikov/Shutterstock.com; pp. 9, 24 fantom_rd/Shutterstock.com; pp. 11, 24 GAyala/Shutterstock.com; p. 13 schankz/Shutterstock.com; p. 15 Ekaterina Pankina/Shutterstock.com; p. 17 Aeksei Lazukov/Shutterstock.com; pp. 19, 24 Sonsedska Yuliia/Shutterstock.com; p. 21 Cynoclub/Shutterstock.com; p. 23 Cher KFM/Shutterstock.com.

Printed in the United States of America

CPSIA compliance information: Batch #CSGS23: For further information contact Gareth Stevens, New York, New York at 1-800-542-2595.

Contents

Cats are popular pets. Their bodies are special.

Cats have two eyes.
They see well
in the dark.

Cats have whiskers.
They feel movement.

A cat's tongue is rough.
Cats lick their bodies.
This is grooming.

Adult cats have 30 teeth. Their teeth cut up food they eat.

A cat has two ears.
They can move around!

Cat bodies bend easily.

They walk on their toes.
Front paws have
five toes.

Most cats have long hair or short hair. Some have no hair!

Most have tails too.

Words to Know

paw

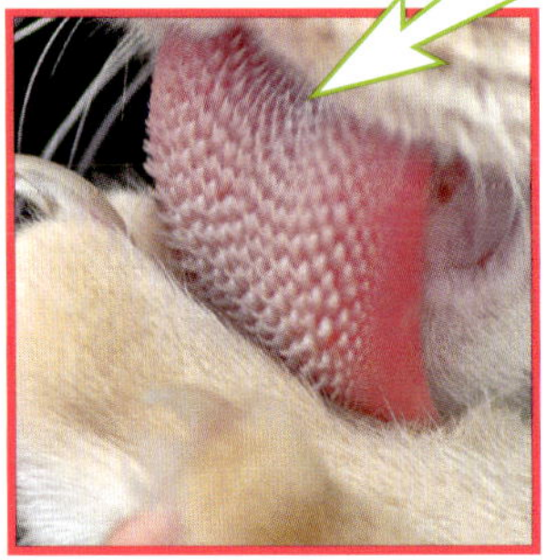
tongue

whiskers

Index